World Book's Learning Ladders

World of Insects

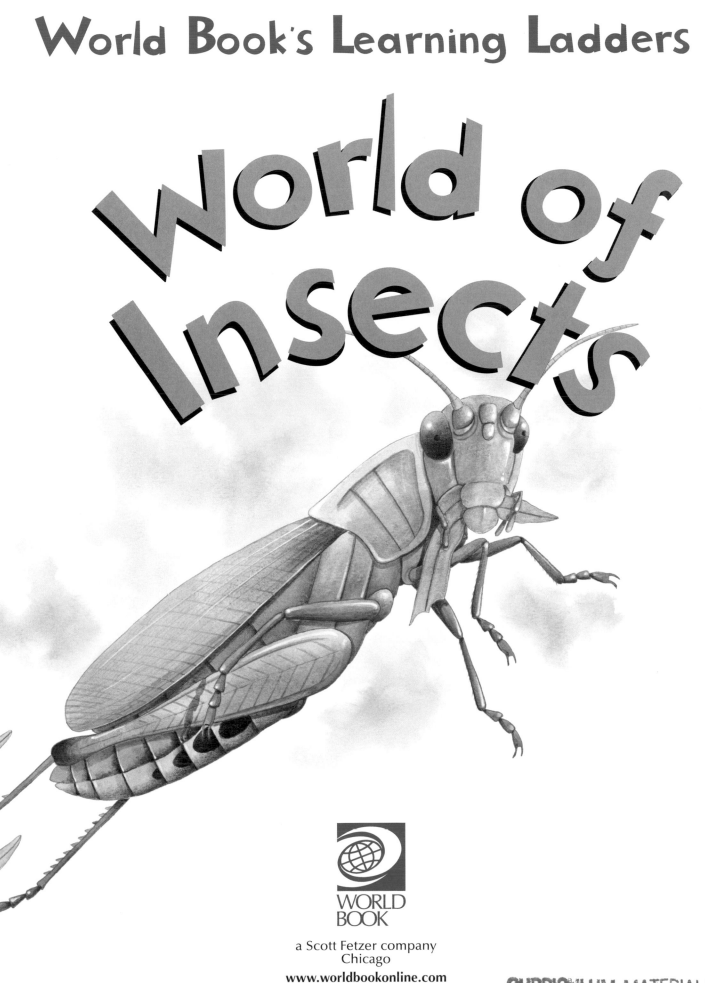

WORLD
BOOK

a Scott Fetzer company
Chicago
www.worldbookonline.com

WORLD BOOK

233 N. Michigan Avenue
Chicago, IL 60601
U.S.A.

For information about other World Book publications, visit our Web site at
http://www.worldbookonline.com or call **1-800-WORLDBK (967-5325).**

For information about sales to schools and libraries, call **1-800-975-3250 (United States);**
1-800-837-5365 (Canada).

Library of Congress Cataloging-in-Publication Data

World of insects.
    p. cm. -- (World Book's learning ladders)
    Summary: "Introduction to insects, using simple
text, question and answer format, illustrations, and
photos. Features include puzzles and games, fun
facts, resource list, and index"--Provided by publisher.
    Includes bibliographical references and index.
    ISBN 978-0-7166-7735-2
    1. Insects--Juvenile literature. I. World Book, Inc.
QL467.2.W676 2007
595.7--dc22
                                2007019904

World Book's Learning Ladders
Set ISBN: 978-0-7166-7725-3

Printed in China
2 3 4 5 6 12 11 10 09 08

Editor in Chief: Paul A. Kobasa

Supplementary Publications
    Associate Director: Scott Thomas
    Managing Editor: Barbara A. Mayes

Senior Editor: Shawn Brennan

Editor: Dawn Krajcik

Researcher: Cheryl Graham

Manager, Editorial Operations
    (Rights & Permissions): Loranne K. Shields

Graphics and Design
    Associate Director: Sandra M. Dyrlund
    Associate Manager, Design: Brenda B. Tropinski
    Associate Manager, Photography: Tom Evans

Production
    Director, Manufacturing and Pre-Press: Carma Fazio
    Manager, Manufacturing: Steven Hueppchen
    Production Technology Manager: Anne Fritzinger
    Proofreader: Emilie Schrage

This edition is an adaptation of the Ladders series
published originally by T&N Children's Publishing, Inc.,
of Minnetonka, Minnesota.

Photographic credits: Cover: © Ariel Bravy, Shutterstock; p5: NHPA/James Carmichael Jr.; p7: OSF/Mantis
Wildlife Films; p8: Ardea/John Mason; p11: NHPA/Stephen Dalton; p13: OSF/Michael Fogden;
p16: OSF/Terry Button; p19: OSF/Brian Kenney; p20: Naturepl.com/Jose B. Ruiz; p21: OSF;
p23: NHPA/Robert Thompson.

Illustrators: John Eggert, Stephen Holmes, Jon Stuart

What's inside?

This book is about the secret and colorful world of insects. Find out where and how they live, their cunning disguises, and their clever defenses.

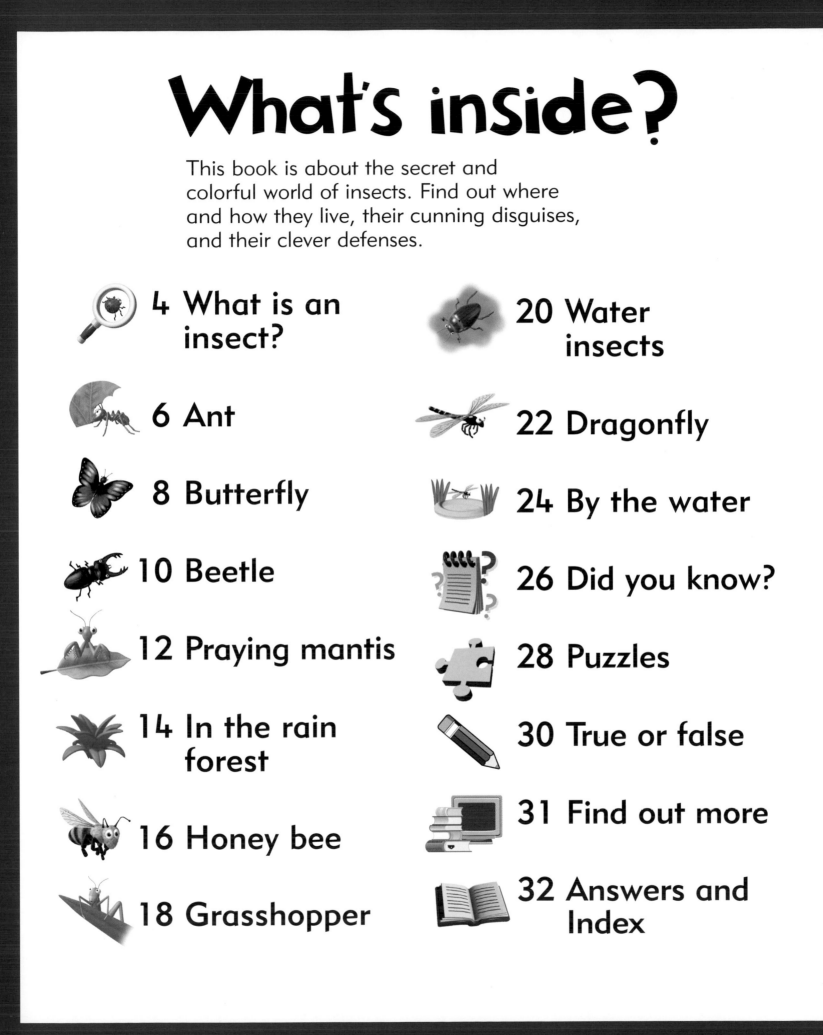

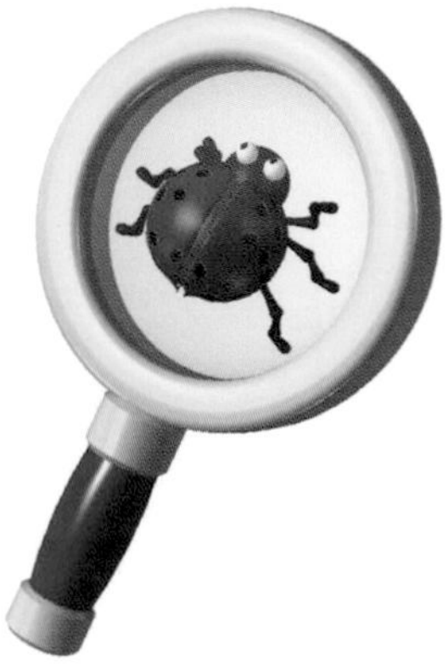

What is an insect?

The tough **cover** on an insect's body protects its soft insides.

There are over 1 million kinds of insects in the world. They are found on land and in the fresh water of lakes and rivers. But they cannot live in salty oceans. An insect has three main body parts: a head, a thorax, and an abdomen. All insects have six legs, and many have wings. Insects can be as large as a football or as small as the period at the end of this sentence. The insect shown here is an ant.

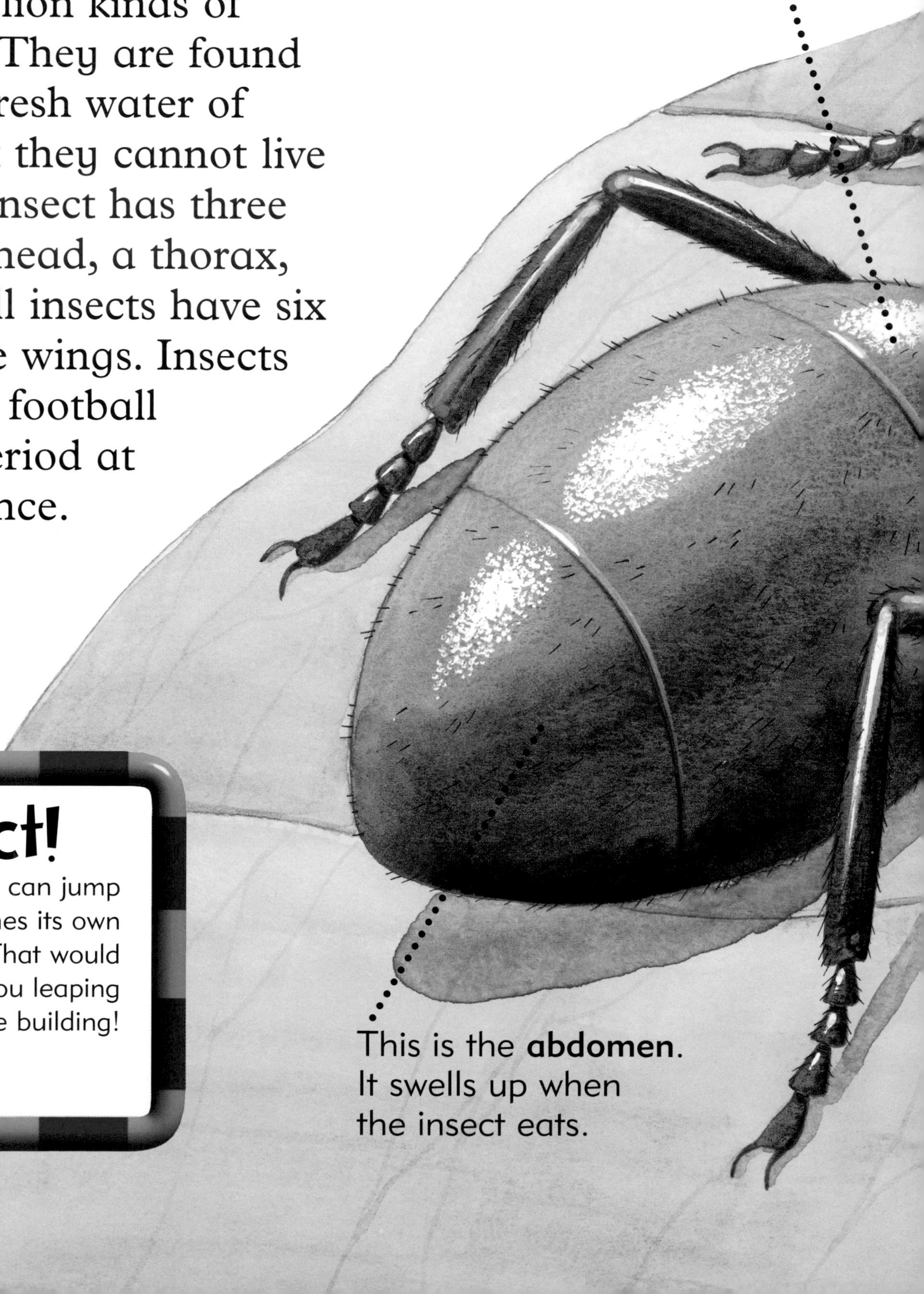

It's a fact!

A tiny flea can jump 100 times its own height. That would be like you leaping over an office building!

This is the **abdomen**. It swells up when the insect eats.

An insect's **head** has eyes and antennae, as well as mouth parts for eating.

Most insects have two long **antennae**. They are used mainly for feeling and smelling.

The middle part of an insect's body is called the **thorax**. The legs are attached there.

Spiders are not insects. A spider has eight legs instead of six, and its body is made up of two parts, not three.

Ant

Lift up a stone or a log, and you will probably see tiny ants scurrying around. There are many different kinds of ants. Most live together in large groups called colonies. Ants work hard as a team, building nests, collecting food, and fighting enemies.

This is a **leaf-cutter ant**. It lives on the damp floor of the rain forest.

This worker is using its strong **jaws** to cut a leaf.

These weaver ants are building a nest. The ants glue leaves together with a silklike material that they spin from their bodies.

Hooked **claws** help the ant cling to slippery branches as it marches home.

A leaf-cutter ant carries a piece of **leaf** back to its underground nest. The leaf will be turned into food.

Butterfly

Most insects can fly. Their wings are attached to their thorax. A butterfly usually has large, colorful wings. Like all insects, the butterfly starts life as a tiny egg, but it goes through many changes before it becomes an adult. The life cycle of a blue morpho butterfly is shown here.

Day 1
A mother butterfly lays a bunch of pale **eggs** on a leaf.

Moths are related to butterflies. But a moth's body is thick and furry. Its antennae look a bit like feathers.

2

Day 9
A **caterpillar** hatches from each egg and starts eating. It feeds on leaves until it is big and fat.

3

Week 8
A hard shell, called a **chrysalis**, forms around the caterpillar.

Week 10
The butterfly's **wings** are crumpled at first, but they soon straighten out. The new butterfly flies off.

4

Week 10
Inside the shell, a butterfly has formed. The shell cracks and the **new butterfly** slowly slides out.

Beetle

There are thousands of different beetles in the world, and they come in many colors, shapes, and sizes. Beetles are tough insects, with hard coverings called wing cases on their backs. Beetles spend much of their time crawling on the ground. They either run or fly away to escape from danger.

Male stag beetles sometimes lock jaws and try to push each other over. They do this to attract females.

This is a male giant **stag beetle**. It can grow to nearly 3 inches (7 ½ centimeters) long.

Like all insects, a beetle always keeps three **legs** on the ground as it walks.

The male stag beetle has huge **jaws** that look a bit like a deer's antlers.

Ladybugs are a helpful type of beetle. They eat pests that feed on garden flowers and farm crops.

A beetle's delicate **wings** are hidden under its wing cases.

Wing case

It's a fact!

A firefly is a type of beetle that makes a flashing or glowing light. The male uses his light to attract a female.

Praying mantis

A praying mantis is a fierce hunter that can measure up to 5 inches (13 centimeters) long. Most live in warm climates. A praying mantis sits perfectly still with its legs folded, waiting for an insect to pass. Then, in a flash, it reaches out and grabs its prey.

A praying mantis can turn its **head** almost all the way around as it looks for food.

This mantis is shooting out its huge front legs to grab a **fly**.

Rows of sharp spikes on each **leg** make it impossible for the prey to escape.

This orchid mantis looks like part of the flower on which it is hiding. This helps the mantis to catch insects.

When a praying mantis is resting, its **wings** lie flat on its back.

In the rain forest

Rain forests are hot, steamy places where it rains often. Plants grow quickly here, and they provide food and shelter for many types of insects. The insects shown here all live close to the rain forest floor.

14

Words you know

Here are words that you read earlier in this book. Say them out loud, then find the things in the picture.

praying mantis   stag beetle

butterfly eggs   leaf-cutter

blue morpho   ants

butterfly

15

Honey bee

In summer, a honey bee spends its day flying from flower to flower, collecting a sugary liquid called nectar. The bee takes the nectar back to its hive and then turns it into honey. This will be its winter food. Bees also collect a dust called pollen from flowers to feed the baby bees in the hive.

A honey bee beats its **wings** so fast that it makes a buzzing noise as it flies.

Wasps are related to bees. Like bees, wasps have bright stripes to warn other animals to stay away.

A sharp **stinger** is useful for fighting off enemies.

Fine **hairs** all over the honey bee's body pick up the pollen.

These parts of the flower, called the **stamens,** are covered in yellow pollen.

To carry the pollen home, the bee brushes it into areas on its back legs called **baskets**.

It's a fact!

When a honey bee finds food, it tells the other bees where to go by performing a special dance.

Grasshopper

Most grasshoppers live in fields and meadows, where there are plenty of plants to eat. Although they have wings, not all grasshoppers can fly. When some grasshoppers spot an enemy, such as a frog, they jump high into the air to escape. There are over 20,000 types of grasshoppers.

A grasshopper rubs its back legs against its front **wings** to make a chirping sound. It does this to attract a mate.

Powerful back **legs** help a grasshopper to push itself off the ground.

Crickets are related to grasshoppers. The field cricket's song changes according to the weather. The hotter it gets, the faster the cricket chirps.

The grasshopper's **lip** hides strong jaws for chewing leaves and biting enemies.

A grasshopper's **color** and markings help to make this insect blend in well with its surroundings.

A katydid is a type of grasshopper. It gets its name from the noise it makes, which sounds like "katydid-katydid."

Water insects

Many insects live in or near water, where food is plentiful and there are many places to hide from enemies. Here, a large diving beetle is plunging deep into the water to look for food. It carries a bubble of air under its wing cases so it can breathe.

A large **diving beetle** can measure up to 1½ inches (4 centimeters) long.

A flattened **body** helps the beetle move quickly.

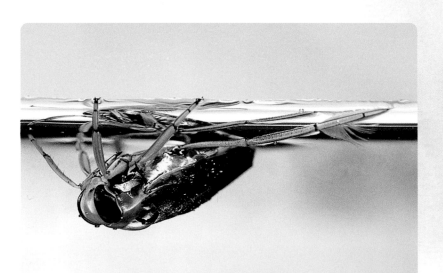

Backswimmers swim upside down. They lie on their backs and use their back legs like oars to move along.

A pond **snail** makes a tasty snack for the diving beetle.

The beetle's hairy back **legs** are shaped like paddles. The beetle uses them to swim through the water.

A water strider can run across water on its long, skinny back legs. It uses its two front legs to grab other insects to eat.

Hooks at the ends of the **feet** are useful for clinging to slippery underwater plants.

It's a fact!

Baby diving beetles look very different from their parents, but they are just as fierce. They use their big jaws to snap at tadpoles.

Dragonfly

Colorful dragonflies often are found near streams and ponds. They are fast fliers, and they can fly up, down, forward, and backward. They can even hover, or stay in one place in the air, like a helicopter! Dragonflies hunt in the air by darting out to grab other flying insects.

Huge **eyes** help a dragonfly spot its insect prey.

A tiny **mosquito** is a favorite meal for dragonflies.

A dragonfly holds out its **legs** as it flies, making a net to catch its food.

A long, thin **body** helps the dragonfly balance as it darts around.

Four large, delicate **wings** allow the insect to hover.

The damselfly is related to the dragonfly. It lives underwater at the start of its life and on land when it is fully grown.

23

By the water

All insects need water to drink, food to eat, and a safe place to hide from enemies. This river is home to many different insects. Some are looking for food in the plants that grow next to the river. Others are flying overhead.

24

What is the dragonfly trying to catch?

Words you know

Here are words that you read earlier in this book. Say them out loud, then find the things in the picture.

honey bee   dragonfly
grasshopper   water striders
mosquito   diving beetle

Which insects are moving across the water on their long legs?

Did you know?

The word *butterfly* comes from an old English word meaning "butter-colored flying creature." Because yellow butterflies were common in England, this name became the English name for all of these insects.

Airplane pilots have seen monarch butterflies flying more than 10,000 feet (3,000 meters) above the ground!

Some kinds of grasshoppers smell really bad—and that's good! Their rotten odors keep their enemies away!

A cricket can clean itself while it sings.

The honey bee is the state insect of 10 states: Arkansas, Maine, Mississippi, Missouri, New Jersey, Oklahoma, South Dakota, Utah, Vermont, and Wisconsin.

It takes 80,000 fireflies to make the same amount of light made by one candle.

Beetle blood may be yellow, green, or orange.

Some ants can survive up to 14 days underwater!

Puzzles

Close-up!

We've zoomed in on parts of some insects' bodies. Can you figure out which insects you are looking at?

1

2

3

Answers on page 32.

Follow me!

Can you figure out what the dragonfly, praying mantis, and great diving beetle will eat for their dinner? Follow the lines to find out!

dragonfly   praying mantis   diving beetle

pond snail   mosquito   fly

Match up!

Match each word on the left with its picture on the right.

1. butterfly

2. ant

3. grasshopper

4. honey bee

5. beetle

6. praying mantis

a

b

c

d

e

f

Answers on page 32.

True or false

Can you figure out which of these statements are true? Turn to the page numbers given to help you find the answers.

3 The female firefly flashes her light on and off to attract a male. **Go to page 11.**

1 A flea can jump more than 500 times its own height. **Go to page 4.**

2 A honey bee beats its wings so fast that it makes a buzzing sound as it flies. **Go to page 16.**

4 A grasshopper makes a chirping sound with its mouth. **Go to page 18.**

5 Tadpoles feast on baby diving beetles. **Go to page 21.**

Answers on page 32.

Find out more

Books

Beetles, Kathleen Derzipilski (Benchmark Books, 2005)
Find out how to recognize different kinds of beetles, where they live, and how they grow from babies to adults.

Bug Books, Jill Bailey, Karen Hartley, Chris Macro, and Philip Taylor (Heinemann Library, 2006) 12 volumes
Each book focuses on a different kind of insect, such as centipedes, cockroaches, and ladybugs. Especially helpful are the close-up photos and the diagrams showing the parts of each insect's body.

Bug Safari, Bob Barner (Holiday House, 2004)
Follow a boy as he explores his backyard and finds 16 different insects.

From Caterpillar to Butterfly, Anita Ganeri (Heinemann Library, 2006)
Watch a butterfly develop from its birth to adulthood.

The Life Cycle of Insects, Louise and Richard Spilsbury (Heinemann Library, 2003)
Insects mate, have babies, and grow up to become adults in a variety of ways, which you will see in this book.

Web sites

Amazing Insects, by Koday's Kids at Ivy Hall School, Buffalo Grove, Illinois
http://www.ivyhall.district96.K12.il.us/4TH/KKHP/1insects/bugmenu.html
Choose from some 50 insects on the menu and up pop photos and facts about your choice.

Bugbios, by Dexter Sear
http://insects.org/index.html
This Web site is full of close-up photos of many kinds of insects, especially butterflies.

Bugs and Butterflies, by Kaboose
http://resources.kaboose.com/kidslinks/critters/bugs-and-butterflies/
Bugs_and_Butterflies.html
Explore the Internet for cool links on insects—from "Antboy's Bugworld" to "Wendell's Yucky Bug World"—all listed on this single Web site.

Bugs – Insects 4 Kids, by Ann Zeise, A to Z Home's Cool Homeschooling
http://homeschooling.gomilpitas.com/explore/bugs.htm
This resource center has a huge number of links to a wide range of Web sites about insects, listed under such categories as "Bug Arts and Crafts," "Collecting," and "Games."

Insects, Enchanted Learning
http://www.enchantedlearning.com/themes/insects.shtml
Learn about insects through crafts, quizzes, games, drawings, and diagrams.

Answers

Puzzles
from pages 28 and 29

Close-up!
1. honey bee
2. caterpillar chrysalis
3. stag beetle

Match up!
1. c
2. f
3. d
4. e
5. b
6. a

True or false
from page 30

1. false
2. true
3. false
4. false
5. false

Index